DEAR

King

CAN I FIX YOUR TILTED CROWN?

TYNESHA MCCARTY

Published by Divine Oak Publishing
PO BOX 8681
Waukegan, IL 60079

ACKNOWLEDGMENTS

I would first like to thank my Father, God, for giving me such a fantastic gift. A special thanks to all of the people that assisted me in bringing this project to life. I appreciate you all so much. To all of the Kings and Queens that blessed this project with their love, encouraging words, and mini love letters. Without you, our Kings would not get a chance to feel your passion along with your endearing words.

A special thank you to those that sat up and listened as I read and bounced off my ideas to them, as well as any and everyone that has supported me on this writing journey in any shape, form, or fashion.

This book is dedicated to any man that has been stereotyped, broken, or is just in need of a little bit of love and encouragement. I love you, Black King!

INTRODUCTION

King Renown Your Crown

My heart aches as I realize the battle many of us have when uplifting the black man. I first want to say; I HAVE BEEN USED, BROKEN, DISRESPECTED AND BETRAYED BY MANY BLACK MEN. However, it has no bearing on the strong Black King(s); he understands how to treat a woman, father children, respect and honor his mother, and show love to people overall. All while they fight the world out there. It doesn't take away from your beautiful melanin sons and brothers or any other inspiring Black Kings that we see doing the opposite of what society expects from them. From many directions, rage binds many along with misplaced hurt from our own experiences; in turn, we refuse to uplift the Black Kings that love everything about us. We don't acknowledge their beauty, understand their excellence, or recognize their power or even respect them until they are taken off this earth by the hands of someone else.

Only then does their lives matter to us?

Only then does it serve them to scream and march and celebrate them?

If not, now when?

I choose today!

Today, it's time to see the beauty in them in this era, empower them to be better, speak life into them regardless of what lens you viewed them from yesterday! Your words, your energy, your love can

1

uplift a Black King broken beyond measure. Black King, Can I fix your tilted crown, is intended to do just that!

Here, I will give you the love and commemoration you deserve genuinely and empathetically; I will affirm you, speak life into you and share insights from Kings that look just like you and Queens that love you too. We all know the strength and resilience in a black man; Black King, you are powerful! You are a work of art and loved beyond measures; as your Queen, I will continue to support, uplift, and cherish you; in exchange, you must promise those that believe in you that when you walk into your Kingdom, you will be worthy of the attention you command.

DEAR BLACK KING POEM

Dear Black King,
Can I fix your tilted crown?
Can I be the one to help you up when the world has torn you down?

Dear Black King,
Can I hold you and wrap my arms around your build?
Give you love on the days that you have no more to give

Dear King,
Can I be the one you run to? Can I be your closest friend?
The one that keeps your darkest secrets, the one you can confide in?

Dear Black King,
You are so beautiful, and I mean it in every way. No one can replicate
your cadence and the way you continue to slay! Or should I say;kill the
game.
That's neither here nor there. King, all acclamation is the same.

Dear King,
I cheer for you.
at night, I fear the sirens and lights,
and that's when I shed a tear for you!

King,

You are brilliant
Every day you slay the fire-breathing dragons of the world
and King, that makes you resilient!
You take down the giants.
No need to fall in line or get in compliance.

King,

You are exhilarating!
And even when I don't like you,
 the world without you would be devastating.

Dear Black King

I respect you;
they portray you in ways that distort your image; they will never get you.
But I do!

King,

I love everything about you. But you have to know; that even when all odds are against you, that doesn't mean you can't grow!

King,

It's time! To walk into your Kingdom and rise.
Don't let the past hold you back;
they fear you and fight against you with lies and demise.

Stand up, King!
You are a champion, and they know it!
No more time for justifications; put in the work and show it!
When the chances are against you, it's up to you to beat it.
I have yet to meet a man better than the Black Man.

A King, Undefeated!

I LOVE YOU, BLACK KING! ~ *Tynesha* ~

DEAR BLACK KING, YOU ARE A CHILD OF GOD!

*I'm 36 now. If I could say one thing to the twenty-five-year-old me, I would tell him to follow God. For me, that alone has been the most pivotal and critical decision I have ever made. Like many others, my life was riddled with decisions made out of ego, hurt, selfishness, and ignorance passed on to me and perpetuated by more ignorance, a terrible cycle. I lacked growth and didn't even know it. However, upon choosing to follow God in 2017, He has enhanced **every** area in my life in ways unimaginable. It is as if my life was like a house, and as I welcomed Him through the front door, He was patient and compassionate towards the messes that He discovered. And what was good, He made great. Every room of the house that I brought Him in to was left better than the way He found it; the room of relationships, finances, purpose, manhood, business. Things are moving, growing. And as I am still growing, there may be rooms that I am a bit apprehensive or inconsistent about allowing Him into, whether it be because of fear of disappointing Him or just plain old habitual sin that can be tough to break out of. But I am encouraged to seek Him every day, in all things, not only by the work He has already done in my life but by the promises in His Word and the testimonies of those around me. I am a miracle because of Him. And so are you.*

~Kenneth Ledford~

> To my Black Kings, if you have not learned how to put God first, then make this your primary focus. God will direct your path and your load will become a little less heavy.
>
> ~Latoya Hume~s

King,

If you look at what a child represents, you will see the semblance of how you, as a child of God, receive nurture through God figuratively. That is who grows you, matures you, manages you, and takes care of you. If you look at a child in the natural sense, they endeavor to be so independent and take on all these things without knowing what they are doing. Here, you are just the same as children, trying to do it all on your own, and you don't have to. You are a child of God with a plan already laid out for you. The plan fails if you don't first follow him. Don't leave these words; let these words be a platform for you and a North Star. "For I know the plans I have for you," declares the LORD, "plans to prosper you and not to harm you, plans to give you hope and a future. *Jeremiah 29:11*

King, I love you, and I, too, would like to share my testimony with you here. Many women were hesitant about adding an assertion in this manuscript to you, the amazing King which you are. But see Black King, the above passage, was written by one of many Black men that inflicted hurt and pain upon me as a Black Queen. Not only do I have the power of forgiveness, but he has reached a point in which he seeks someone far more powerful than him and has unlocked doors to his Monarchy in return—growth, along with forgiveness from the Kingdom in exchange for restoration. The power of accountability and forgiveness is so beautiful, and the reward connected; unity, friendship, compassion, and understanding. King (s), I want you to know that I love you so much and appreciate your allowing me the opportunity to speak to you as you embark on an empowering journey into your Kingdom. Always know that no weapon formed against you shall prosper.

You are a child of God

Today's Exercise:

Hey King,

Take this day and ask for forgiveness for anything that has you bound; forgive yourself and make things right with your past. All debts must be repaid, accept your role in it, and make amends.

SAY THIS OUT LOUD AND BELIEVE IT:

"I WILL RIGHT MY WRONGS
I FORGIVE MYSELF
I AM RESTORED…"

DEAR BLACK KING, ADJUST YOUR CROWN; YOU ARE THE KING OF YOUR KINGDOM

"The ultimate measure of a man is not where he stands in moments of comfort and convenience, but where he stands at times of challenge and controversy." M.L.K~

Dear King,

I recognize that you are a strong human being with much to offer and are sick and tired of being disrespected in society by your children and spouses, all while trying to withstand the drawbacks of disparities. I realize that you are fed up with not having prospects within society, efficiently, and personally within your own people. Dissension and fight are attached to your history, but so is a triumph and change. Which direction will you choose, and how will you go about getting there?

King, may I take a second first to say, you matter, and you are needed. Why do I even care? Why do you even matter to me? I care because the fundamental nature of all of who you are offers life to my soul. You are the head and not the tail; you are the protector, where it all begins. When I look at the Black man, I see a king who resides in each of them. Some have nurtured this King, and some have abandoned him. Today, I am here to tell you that it is of the utmost importance to your Blackness, melanin, and history do not obliterate your value. My King, royalty, is in your DNA. They fear you because, amid the relentless weight on your shoulders, restraints around your feet, and knees on your neck, you still soar! Even when they try to tilt your crown, you effortlessly readjust it. It is time to unlock the King deep down inside of you that has been locked away and unveil the unequivocal titan that has been retreating. The world without you is unconscious.

YOU ARE THE KING OF YOUR KINGDOM!

Today's Exercise:

Hey King,

I want you to know that your resilience and perseverance are unmatched. Declare freedom over your life today. You inherit the inclination to conquer any barrier. You are a King, a brother, a son, a father, and a lover. You are necessary for our lives. As a Black Queen, I am here to help fix your tilted crown.

SAY THIS OUT LOUD AND BELIEVE IT:

"I AM INNOVATIVE
I AM CHOSEN!
I AM A KING!"

DEAR BLACK KING, YOU ARE A MASTERPIECE!

You are more than what some refrain from measuring; it's not where you stand in moments of triumph and achievement but where you stand in moments of trials and controversy that depict who you are. Let us own our greatness because that's who we are destined to be "Great" and a force to be reckoned with my Black Kings.
~Dre Sincere~

Dear Black King,

As a woman, mother, sister, and daughter, I have had my encounters with Black Men. Good, bad, or indifferent; I love every part of him. I adore him, and I admire him. Every man is not a king. However, every man is not a man. So how do we know? How do we know when a king has surfaced? We do not! Everyone's perception is different; we all don't see through the same lens. One thing we can all recognize, admittedly or not is, Black Men are God's Masterpiece.

Yes! There is something about a Black King that evokes superiority, shakes rooms, and bring about this aura that no other man could. His walk, his talk, his confidence, and that bit of arrogance mixed with humility. There is something about a Black Man that he is the smartest man in the room when he puts his mind to something. His voice demands authority, his posture and existence as a whole passionately bring about an unreplicated aura. I don't know if you know this or not, but you are beautiful. The highest took his time in making you. Everything about you brings about a celestial beauty that the world fails to appreciate at times. I appreciate your existence, and I understand you.

King, let me remind you that your existence is beyond measure. Your presence is divine; you are perfectly made and one of a kind. You are strong and uniquely beautiful. You are loved, exceptional, and are not defective. You are not weird, and you are not a lost cause.

YOU ARE A MASTERPIECE!

Today's Exercise:

Hey King,

Who are you? No, really, who do you see when you look in the mirror?

Today, I was hoping you could look in the mirror and affirm to yourself.

SAY THIS OUT LOUD AND BELIEVE IT
"I AM A MASTERPIECE!
I AM CREATED IN HIS IMAGE.
I AM DIVINE!"

DEAR BLACK KING, YOU ARE RESILIENT

I think the number one issue is society's expectations of black men is; it's all over the place. One minute they want excellence and royal behavior, and then the next, they don't give them the respect that comes with that expectation when they reach those lofty goals. I also believe black men must be bulletproof emotionally and not allowed to "feel" as a human should; this creates a built-up pressure cooker of emotions that, once released, paints us in light of either being uber aggressive or uber soft.

~Navi Robins~

"WE GOT TURNED DOWN, WE FAILED, HAD SETBACKS, HAD TO START OVER A LOT OF TIMES. BUT WE KEPT GOING AT IT. IN ANYBODY'S CASE THAT'S ALWAYS THE DISTINGUISHING FACTOR."

NIPSEY HUSSLE

Dear Black King,

Through decades you have been at war with the world as circumstances had you oppressed. Those that appeardangry are really fearful. Therefore, you have been under attack. You innate strength, tenacity, and shuffle with resilience. Day after day, night after night; you refuse to give up. You fight a battle that no one knows but you. The culmination of constrained social reward has become a driving fuel of your perseverance; I understand the limitation, the surmounted amount of pressure ascended on your shoulders. Many may never understand it, recognize it, or even acknowledge it. But I do, and I could never diminish your beauty, curtail your strength, or dismantle your existence.

The ramification of oppressing the Black Man brought about a message that demanded a new social shift level that frightened the oppressor. The Black Man continues to thrive and fight for his people. The picture of him has been distorted, stigmatizing the Black King as violent and aggressive. He has been stereotyped, deceived, lied on, and trained to fight since the beginning of time. Through it all, he stands firm in his power and will not be moved nor scared easily. No matter how grim, there has yet to be a force powerful enough to stunt or conquer the Black Man.

YOU ARE RESILIENT!

Today's Exercise:

Dear Black King,

I, We, Us...LOVE YOU! Do not give up...

Today, I was hoping you could take a second and reflect on all that you have endured. Guess what? You are still here! Today is the day to tell yourself how powerful you are.

SAY THIS OUT LOUD AND BELIEVE IT:

"I AM A GOD!
I AM A MASTER IN ALL THAT I DO.
I AM IN CONTROL OF MY FATE!"

DEAR BLACK KING, YOU HAVE PURPOSE

Search desperately of your past, your ancestors in TRUTH OF ORIGIN, and apply your Homage, discipline, and love to them to find our inner King. To bring it out and live as such.
~David Richardson~

Dear Black King,

You have a purpose. You are worth more than you could imagine. You are a King that can move mountains with the tip of your finger. You are in full control of your Kingdom; all you must do is believe in yourself. A King crafted with care and precision; born into royalty, and unrightfully removed from your throne. It is time to fix your crown and step back into the role meant for you. The position that those before you fought for and laid down and died for. Nothing about you was an accident; you are not who they say you are, but who you believe you are. Your mistakes do not define you, and the trauma and pain no longer have jurisdiction over your life. Never forget, there is purpose over your life and clarity in your next move. So, get there!

No matter how tough the journey gets, how hard the road ahead appears to be, you must know you were purposefully created. You have so much purpose, and your life is worth living. You are so valuable; you are tenacious, determined, loved, and worthy of abundance and happiness and will endure above it all, all because…

YOU HAVE PURPOSE!

Today's Exercise:

Hey King,

It is time to step into your purpose. Acting the part is one thing; you must look the part. Push yourself; no one else will do it for you. Mistakes are proof that you are trying.

Take some time out of your day and write out the things that you want in life. Create an action plan and proceed to manifest what it is that belongs to you. It's time to reclaim your throne and step into your purpose.

SAY THIS OUT LOUD AND BELIEVE IT:

"I AM SUCCESSFUL!
I AM WEALTHY!
I HAVE A PURPOSE."

DEAR BLACK KING, YOU ARE OPEN!

I remember him looking into my eyes with such an aching. He had been so tough for so long, yet the weight of the world had come crashing down on him, and there was nothing he could do to stop it. As tough as he was, he was still human. When a tear kissed his face, one kissed mine as well, creating a downpour of tears that had been blocked and restricted. Some women may have looked at him as feeble and weak. But to me, there was a beauty in his vulnerability that urged me to hold him as I would want him to hold me. I assured him that it was okay, and I allowed him to open up to me without conviction.

~Tynesha~

"Your vulnerability is just as beautiful as your masculinity."

~Shaquita Monique~

Dear Black King,

Did you know that vulnerability does not make you weak? It has no bearing on your manhood, and to a woman, a real woman, it is the most beautiful thing you can disclose. Balance is everything, and it is necessary. There is nothing wrong with being open; vulnerability is natural to a certain extent. It is okay to have a safe space as you assure yourself that no one tries to take this time as an opportunity to take advantage of the situation. This is an opportunity to appreciate it. Vulnerability is not a weakness; it is a key to self-expression. It is okay; you are human!

The Black Man is not immune to trauma; history and data indicate that trauma is considerably higher amongst Black males. Emotional well-being is a subject matter that is often omitted in Black culture, but the Black Man was raised to keep his chin up, man up, and find courage as if crying makes him less than. Many times, we associate our need for emotional expression with a form of softness. The Blackman is expected to withstand anything, and although he is a resilient being, his state of mind must have a healthy balance.

King,

As a young man, you were told not to cry; today, the world around you wonders why you are now insensitive to the women who desire sensitivity from a man. Black Man, you have been told that it is not okay to show emotions while carrying the weight of the world. How quickly we forget the apprehensions that some Black Men hold due to their Black skin. Something happened here, somewhere; somehow, they forgot that you, too, are an emotional being. That emotional side of you was pushed way down deep in the basement, creating a hardcore individual, lacking compassion.

I am here to reassure you that nothing about a man's emotional expression is taboo; emotional pain is valid. Holding back tears does not make you stronger or more of a man. It is now time to reject the unnecessary labels and seizing of the manifestos that depict it a crime to be a Black and vulnerable man in this society. I want to encourage you to allow yourself space to be vulnerable. It is not weak to love, express love, and to give love.

DON'T EVER CLOSE; ALWAYS REMAIN OPEN!

Today's Exercise:

Hey King,

When was the last time you cried, a cry that you could feel as you allowed yourself to feel the endorphins released from your body? Today, I want you to allow yourself room to be vulnerable. Take this time to express love and to give love.

SAY THIS OUT LOUD AND BELIEVE IT:

"I AM OPEN;
I AM BRAVE!
I AM ENOUGH!"

DEAR BLACK KINGS, YOU ARE A LEADER

Everything begins with you; we need you to be grounded and protected by something far beyond what the eyes can see. It is time to expose our children to things that are linked to effects that better help them overcome the most critical challenges. In many of our communities, we are riddled with misdirection, gang violence, and imbalance in the family; As leaders, it is time to expose our children and families to things that will break away from many challenges we consistently face.

~Kenneth Ledford~

Assume your position!

You have Queens who are waiting for you to lead; we need you just as much as you need us. Kings elevate so that your Queen can take her position beside you.

~Monique Domino~

Dear Black Kings,

Don't believe what the world out there says. After all, what do "they" know anyhow? Black Queen's love and desire Black Kings. The world aims to destroy and infiltrate your mind and belief system with misinformation; we are against and are on a strong search for a man outside of our own. The stories that they tell have no truth here. Why would we settle for anything less than a King when the whole world also desires and yearns for our Black Kings? We have no intent on leaving our Black Kings, and we are waiting for you to tap in.

My King, did you know that your leadership could impact every aspect of so many lives? With the social injustice that we have before us today, it is more important now than ever to have strong leaders in our community. It is even more important to hold the leadership we have accountable. You matter, and I want to be part of your growth, lifting your head high and breaking the generational stigmas placed upon you. My forsaken King that is *my* why! I adore how you are not fearful of rising for your family and that exclusive way that you demonstrate how much you love us. I watch in awe of your ability not to allow statistics to establish your path to excellence!

YOU ARE A LEADER!

Today's Exercise:

Today is your day to take the lead in your life. No, really! Anyone can delegate tasks, but leadership comes with more; it's connected to having a significant impact on those around you. Make those around you better!

SAY THIS OUT LOUD AND BELIEVE IT:
"I ATTRACT PROSPERITY.
I AM DEVOTED!
I AM A LEADER!"

DEAR BLACK KING, YOUR VOICE IS POWERFUL

Black Brother, it is time to give uplifting messages of unity. Help your brother up, don't tear him down. Don't always look to take advantage of someone who looks like you. Demand the same standard you do from your brother from everyone else, don't kill your brother over a dollar and let the white man walk off unscathed with thousands of dollars from you; "be your brother's keeper" should be a lifestyle, not a hashtag.

~Dipo~

Dear King,

You can influence people without trying to control them. You have a voice that demands attention. Use it to empower and uplift. Though silence can sometimes be loud, silence can also be a lie when you have something to say. Your silence is not a part of your divine creation; your design requires you to resonate past fences and attain the things many can't. You have the power to push and endure under any restrictions; this is who you are and have been for centuries.

King, you are the voice of the people. You are a leader amid those that lack the lens to view your ability to lead. Your resilience, ingenuity, and competence to reign as a leader through doubt are part of your build and structure. You are that CEO that challenges minds, that business partner that inherent vital elements of effective management. You are responsible, straight forward, and have no desire to quit because you are a boss. A boss that stands on his truth and has no trouble addressing what's right. You are fully aware that as a king,

YOUR VOICE IS POWERFUL.

Today's Exercise:

Today is your day to take the lead in your life. No, really! Anyone can delegate tasks, but leadership comes with more; it significantly impacts those around you. Make those around you better!

SAY THIS OUT LOUD AND BELIEVE IT:
"I HAVE A VOICE.
I AM A BOSS!
I EMBRACE CHANGE!"

DEAR BLACK KING, YOU ARE RESPECTED

A Black man can use respect, not just from the world he fights against but also from his Queen. Drive to push him to be better and set standards that are above mediocracy. Nurture and understand that she is equal. However, that doesn't mean she competes with him; if I have to compete with my woman, I'm out! We should be a team, not adversaries.

~Navi Robins~

The sun himself is weak when he first rises, and gathers strength and courage as the day gets on.

-Charles Dickens

Hello King,

Being Black is no heinous crime you chose to commit, and it's not anything you should ever have to apologize for. You do not have to apologize for who you are; making others feel safe for their discrepancies is not your responsibility. You don't have to look down at your shoes as she clutches her purse or make someone else comfortable for your existence. You are to be congratulated for your accomplishments, loved for your dominance, and be proud of yourself for being a Black Man.

King, respect is a two-way street, but for some odd reason, there is a lack thereof when it comes to what you look like versus who you are. I know the lack of respect from others can make you feel powerless at times. This is what "they" want. King; they are fully aware that psychological invalidation is one of the most lethal forms of emotional abuse. It destroys confidence, creativity, and individuality. We will not let that happen to you. I am here to tell you; I respect you! Don't let their energy change yours; stand up, King! You have risen amid the whips and chains, surpassed their ignorant thoughts and manipulative ways. Stand up, King; you have graduated past the nigger they labeled you to be.

YOU ARE RESPECTED

Today's Exercise:

Your abilities are to build something lasting; you want respect for your contribution. Today is your day to demand your respect and take the front seat in walking in a standard that sets the tone to be treated like the King that you are. Be the person you want others to see you as, treat yourself and others with respect. Make it a habit to respect those even when you feel they don't deserve it!

SAY THIS OUT LOUD AND BELIEVE IT:

"I AM DILIGENT!
I HAVE THE POWER TO MAKE A DIFFERENCE!
I HAVE OTHERS DEPENDING ON ME TO WIN!"

DEAR BLACK KING, YOU ARE ESSENTIAL

The problem with systemic racism is that many still seek acceptance from people who will never value us, and it's a poor excuse for not standing up! When you understand and believe in your power, you will create and build for yourself. Education gives you that power. The challenges of our grandfathers and their fathers were far more restrictive, but they forged ahead anyway. The strength of who we are as a people is in the power of family and education.

~Glenda Sthurghill~

King,

My amazing King, it is essential that you know that you are indispensable first and foremost! More important than you know. You are brave, courageous, and tough. You are a warrior, and you are worth it! I support you. You are not alone. I apologize for how the world can make you feel and think less of yourself. Just know you are loved! You are a King! Change your thoughts, and your thoughts can change your world!

My Dear King,

As valuable as you are, invest in yourself in all that you do. Educate yourself, expose yourself to people that are trying to better themselves and if you are already on that path, pour into someone that is not. Always know that no matter how many mistakes you make or how slow you progress, you are still way ahead of everyone who isn't trying. You are and will always be more than what they think you are!

AMP UP or get left behind, King.

You Are Essential!

Today's Exercise:

Today and every day moving forward, I want you to understand that you are far more important than many people would like to admit. Never doubt your own value and worthiness.

SAY THIS OUT LOUD AND BELIEVE IT:

"I AM RELIABLE,
I AM IMPORTANT,
I HAVE ALREADY WON."

DEAR BLACK KING, YOU ARE A ROLE MODEL!

"Our Black men are men of power and strength. They embody manhood. They are creative, skillful, intelligent, bold, and a force to be reckoned with. This is why they are seen as a threat; they are a Gold mine !! I love our black men because you are our rock and our covering next to God; you are the most highly esteemed and respected. This is why we need you so much. I'm honored to be a daughter to a black king, a lover to a black king, a sister to a black king, and a mother to black kings!

~Amber Harris~

We need more fathers/role
models in our lives

~Charnita McCarty~

King,

Who, do you serve? Who do you live for aside from yourself? When I think of the role model in the Black Man, I see a man that gives hope and inspiration to people in their lives.

King, you are mimicked in all things by all cultures for the most part. The way you walk, the way you talk, through your creativity and ability to lead effortlessly. As a role model, you have no problem owning up to your mistakes, for you know that mistakes are a part of life. You recognize the impact you have on those around you, and you can gauge your readiness to shift with an open mind.

My Dear King,

Oh, how I love the manner you maneuver your way through the weeds and out of the gutter, stepping into greatness by any means. As a role model, I adore how you show love to those around you, give back to your community, and uplift the women in your life through your gift. You know the value of empowerment and how it is unnecessary to tear each other down or invalidate each other's experiences. To love someone is to value them and their experiences and to support them into their own greatness.

You Are A Role Model

Today's Exercise:

Take today and think of the impact your role has on other people in your life. Use this as an opportunity to build on that and keep pushing others to be great. The reward behind that is priceless. I believe in you, King!

SAY THIS OUT LOUD AND BELIEVE IT:
"I AM IMPACTFUL,
I AM GREAT,
I AM FORTUNATE."

DEAR BLACK KING, YOU ARE SELF-SUFFICIENT!

I believe black men need more self-love; more respect for themselves; many tine men act more of their emotions, leading to terrible decisions. They need to be taught how to be responsible. I believe that too many black men don't know how to take care of themselves because they lack a male figure in their lives; with that, their mother overcompensates and aims to give him the world. This results in him growing up and not grasping the concepts of how to care for himself.

~Tasha Washington~

A person learns how to love himself through the simple acts of loving and being loved by someone else.

-Haruki Murakami

King,

Unfortunately, you have to deal with so much chaos in your life from other people that look like you. Even then, you recognize that you don't have to be a thug or an idiot to be

39

adequate. For so long, our people were programmed to believe that getting an education, speaking with intelligence, and staying out of trouble makes you "not black enough." You are knowledgeable and can be as successful as you desire. You are a go-getter, and you are unstoppable.

Black Man, Black Man, look at you, setting goals, creating plans, and disciplining yourself. I see you, King. Amid all those people out there that told you, you couldn't; you did. You don't have to depend on anyone else to reach your goals. You have laid down the law with the man in the mirror and taken down the giant of procrastination, laziness, and co-dependency.

YOU ARE SELF-SUFFICIENT

Today's Exercise:

Get up, King, take down whatever giant you may be facing today. The only one you compete with is yourself. Today is a day to be better than you were yesterday.

SAY THIS OUT LOUD AND BELIEVE IT:

"I AM TRIUMPHANT,
I AM DARING,
I AM RELIABLE."

DEAR BLACK KING, YOU ARE A PROVIDER!

There is this prevalent belief that black men lack the essential skills it takes to care for themselves. Many believe the black men are shiftless, aimless, and have no sense of responsibility. While it is true that many black men may innate these qualities, the reality is, many black men do not. If we look back, black men have been relatively self-sufficient until recent times. Though we were freed and granted equality, we lost sight of what we were working towards; white people do not determine our people's success. We do! Because we stopped working together as a whole, we have become competitive and stagnant.

~Tynesha~

Black King,

There is this sense of exclusivity of the Black Man that I admire. Even through the different challenges and stages of the Black man's life, they can somehow hold onto a piece of themselves that few can access. Even when it appears that the world hates you, you aim to make a way and live in your purpose as a King despite not having all the resources. I love the way you take care of your family and the way you love your Queen. If you want something in this world, you have to work for it! Living, earning, and love is TRUE HUSTLE.

"The Dream is free; the hustle is sold separately."

My King,

I love your grind and how you will do whatever it takes to provide for your family. Your originality, ingenuity, and intellect are intriguing as you piece the puzzles together in your head to make it work. You innate the tenacity and ethic as you work your behind off for your household. There will be times that things will be far more complicated than others, but you, my King, are built to last, and this realization is what makes you extraordinary.

YOU ARE A PROVIDER

Today's Exercise:

Step back for a second king, take a look in the mirror and tell that man how proud you are. Be proud of yourself even when no one else will!

SAY THIS OUT LOUD AND BELIEVE IT:

I AM PRODUCTIVE,
I AM HUNGRY,
I DEFY THE ODDS."

DEAR BLACK KING, YOU ARE A PROTECTOR!

"King, you are my leader, my Sensai, and my protector as I am yours. We are one. Nothing in this realm is greater and more vibrational than my love for you. I hold this space for you in both light & dark and dare anything to stand in my way of that. Namaste"

 *Shaquita Monique* ∞

King,

Consciously and unconsciously, it has always been your mission to be efficient leaders, providers, and protectors. You have been chosen to oversee those that are incapable of protecting themselves. In your nature, it is to be a protector as an individual, husband, father, and in communities even when you have hateful people in this world against you. I am inspired by your innate ability to provide for and protect your family in the face of obstacles and danger. It is amazing how you will do everything in your power to keep those you love and care for safe.

King,

You are more than the nasty things they say about you. As a queen, I can attest that you can and will do more than many have ever envisioned you would. You are the father that will protect his daughter from a broken heart. You are the brother that will uplift his sister when she has been shattered. You are that son that will defend his mother's honor. You are that husband or partner who will move mountains for his wife, and that King will protect all Black queens by all means. You will lay down your life for those that are incapable of defending their own, and for that, I salute you, my King.

YOU ARE A PROTECTOR!

Today's Exercise:

Today I was hoping you could place the needs of others above your desires. Keep at your mission and protect those around you by walking in your quest.

SAY THIS OUT LOUD AND BELIEVE IT:

"I AM VICTORIOUS,
I AM FEARLESS,
I AM A SAFEGUARD FOR OTHERS."

DEAR BLACK KING, YOU ARE LOVED!

"I love the Black Man and everything that comes with him. From the crown of his head to the tips of his toes. Everything feels right when he is right and good to me as a woman. There is no other being in this world that I feel more protected with aside from the Black Man, and for that, I love you, and I always will."

~Whitney Hych~

King,

Allow yourself to be still. Think of all the love that surrounds you amid the lack of love given. You are a prize assembled for greatness. Your beauty is immaculate, and some may never take the time to figure that out. As they spit venom, the Black King faces criticism that he would use, abuse, mistreat, and abandon me as a Queen. I have been on that end; honestly, I have. That will never take away from or diminish the love I have for you, King. I may not like some of the things you do, which is only because I know that you are better than that. You have qualities that many will render to be less than because you are more significant than they are. More prominent than past choices, larger than the rejection. Rejection derived from those who failed to see your value and appreciate your uniqueness. You are above it all, even when you didn't have a fair chance to demonstrate your greatness.

My King,

You are so sophisticated and addictive, so endearing and empathetic even when the world illustrates you as rough and rugged without grace. As a King, you only compare yourself to your highest self and continue to be strong in everything you do. Your love for yourself grounds me, and your push makes me love you far past any limitation. My Dear King, sometimes life takes you in a direction you never saw yourself going, but it turns out to be the best road you have ever taken. You are someone spectacular, and I wish for all of your dreams to come true as you continue to blossom into the man that God ordained you to be. I will always have a love for you. King, you play a significant role in many lives, and I appreciate what I learn and continue to learn from you. Never forget, you are seen. You are valuable.

YOU ARE LOVED.

Today's Exercise:

King,

    You have a blank slate with yourself; the power to surmount the odds and soar past the labels and tied to your title. There may have been something lost inside you that only you can find, only you can unlock, and only you can affirm Love you, no, really love you, because I love you, King!

SAY THIS OUT LOUD AND BELIEVE IT:

"I AM SELF-EFFACING,
I AM A PROUD,
I AM FORTUNATE."

DEAR BLACK KING, YOU ARE COMPASSIONATE!

We must develop and maintain the capacity to forgive. He who is devoid of the power to forgive is devoid of the power to love. There is some good in the worst of us and some evil in the best of us. When we discover this, we are less prone to hate our enemies.

~Martin Luther King Junior~

King,

Compassion derives from many angles. There's something special about a form of compassion that emanates from struggle and understanding. Your experience gives you the perspicacity to demonstrate compassion to others even when you feel they don't deserve it. You recognize what it feels like to have labels and accounts overflowing with pessimism attached to who you are, even when that is *not* who you are. Your Blackness alone is a target even though it should not be. The world we live in lacks compassion and empathy for the Black King because to vilify him is their reality. What a sad truth that is. A reality where they don't see their perspective write out a prescription that doesn't have your name on it; the purpose attached to your name is far more vindicating and fitting for who you are. A dignified King gifted with compassion, saturated in value, and entrenched with nobility.

See King, even when they spraypaint the walls of your house with falsehoods, the author and illustrator of your life will reinstate its value marked with immense exclusivity. There is a level of compassion within you that will not allow those who fail to acknowledge who you are to influence your measures. You rise when they stoop, you stride as they slither, you keep your head held high as they refuse to look you in the eyes. You, King, are something special. You face your confrontations head-on and even still ...

YOU ARE COMPASSIONATE

Today's Exercise:

King,

Today, take the high road and refuse to stoop to any level that is beneath you. Hold nothing against others, don't take it personally, and have the compassion to look through them and see beyond their conflicts; we all are fighting a battle, love them through it.

SAY THIS OUT LOUD AND BELIEVE IT:

"I AM CARING,
I AM THOUGHTFUL,
I AM RECEPTIVE,"

DEAR BLACK KING, YOU ARE SUCCESSFUL!

I agree there is a systematic ploy to keep the black culture from succeeding; however, we have surpassed it in the past and can beat it today.
~Jay Dee Catchings~

Dear Black King,

King, have you ever wondered why society is quick to exploit and recreate a successful black man as soon as he makes one error? They are eager to place you on the chopping block and decapitate every accolade attached to your name. You then become that error, that image, and that is the image society will continue to use to immolate the Successful Black Man. They do this because they know that everything you do comes with greatness; society fears that, and they cannot have a Black Man painted and plastered in this world as who he is. Greatness. They shy away from that image because they know that not only are you already naturally sexy as hell, your success amplifies it.

A Successful Black Man dressed in business attire obscured in a strong sense of self is dangerous, and I love sitting at the edge of my seat, anticipating your next power move. You fly above all of the things meant to tear you down. You have a tunnel vision mentality that will not allow anyone to deter you from where you need to be. I am so in love with the drive you have, and it fuels me to be the best I can be as a Queen. Your success is attached to a level of masculinity that turns me on and makes me love you even more than I already do. King, you do your thing out here in these streets, and I'm proud to be a part of the Kingdom.

YOU ARE A SUCCESSFUL

Today's Exercise:

Today, congratulate yourself on your successes, stepping stones, and accomplishments; even if they appear to be small to you, they play a part in getting to where you need to be. Keep taking steps in the right direction; your success must not be measured by who they want you to be, but by who you are becoming, one brick at a time.

SAY THIS OUT LOUD AND BELIEVE IT:

"I AM EMPOWERED,
I AM SUCCESSFUL,
I AM WALKING INTO PURPOSE."

DEAR BLACK KING, YOU ARE NEEDED!

"As a mother raising two black men, I fear nothing but them losing themselves in this world. It's is my only greatest fear for myself: so many distractions, so much judgment & pressure to be what they see outside of themselves. I would be heartbroken to know and watch my seeds wither away due to the current social climate that pulls at their spirits, chews them up, and spit them out to be a lesser version of self. Everything else I leave the Universe to work out the details for I know & am confident that they are & will always be protected."

~Shaquita Monique~

King,

There is a subtle harmony about a man that does what it takes to keep pushing. However, there is another part that terrifies us and enrages us at the same time. We know that the world will do everything it can to diminish your success as well as your existence, even in your communities. Even then, you are needed. Your presence is unwavering. Your narrative fuel not on who they were, but who you need to be for those who need you.

Emblems of a shameful past will serve no justice to who it is you are today. You are the responsible father, sufficient caregiver, a valuable partner with that inborn capacity to reason without violence as you communicate effectively, respectfully, and without judgment. You are the reason! You give reason!

YOU ARE NEEDED!

DEAR BLACK KING, YOU ARE INNOVATIVE!

I am an entrepreneur, a barber who uses my hands, gifts, and passion for serving others in my community. There is more to me here; I fix cars, I have rn organizations for my community. I don't quit. "I love to work; it feels good to be able to provide for my family. My grandfather gave me a hell of a work ethic and self-preservation. Preserve something for your children. Others' perception of me is none of my business. I come from an environment and upbringing that exposed me to morale and ethics. We are outliving our youth. I notice that not too many black men have jobs, and it seems like the black man has to fight for it.

~Jeff The Barber~

Dear Black King,

It is enlightening to witness the instinctive reactivity that highlights you in every way. I am in awe at the wiring of your mind and how vested you are in your passion. Even as a young boy, your intuitive vision spoke to the young King inside of you. You dreamed big, even when others tried to crush it with the heel of their feet. Your light shines even in the darkness; you don't wither you rise. You give life to the dead, and when you put your mind to something, there is no losing. Even if society doesn't deem you as a winner, you are one because you never stopped.

King, how many times do I have to say, I love you, and I am so proud of you? Your drive, your creativity, and your design. Your DNA comes uniquely wrapped in layers that you may not even recognize; they are there, they are in you; if you have left them there, it's time to go back and get them. You have a gift, a purpose, and a significance to yourself and those around you. I had a King say to me one time, "You have to touch your dream every day." No matter what it is you are doing right now, go there and put your hands on your dream, keep it alive, and it will continue to live through you.

YOU ARE INNOVATIVE

Today's Exercise:

Go back into your childhood, think of that thing or those things you would create and loved to do. You were good at it, too. Are you walking in that, or did something or someone tells you it was far beyond your reach? Think about that, dust off that tucked away passion, and touch it, and if you are already touching it, keep your hand on it and speak life over it today and it will come to fruition. God willing, It is yours, and if it's not in your will, trust me, there is something else down on the inside of you that is.

Go Get It!

SAY THIS OUT LOUD AND BELIEVE IT:

"I AM CREATIVE,
I AM A GO-GETTER,
I AM INGENIOUS"

DEAR BLACK KING, SPEAK IT INTO EXISTENCE!

I remember listening to the radio one day and hearing Biggie say, "Time to get paid/blow up like the World Trade," although this was a reference to the 1993 bombing of the World Trade Center. He did just that, and six years later, 9/11 happens. That part in his song is faded out on many radio stations today. I then began to reflect on other artists such as Kanye, "and when he gets on, he leaves your ass for a white girl." The more I listened, the more I realized that these artists consciously or not spoke things into existence; some have even projected and ascribed to their death through their music. Words have so much power and influence. It's up to you how you use them. Hence, why I'm writing this book, I recognize the power in my words, and I want you to be a vessel in encouraging you to thrive fully and unceasingly.

~Tynesha~

King, Kings, and Kings in the Making.

You are who you think you are and what you say you are. Your voice, that power, that heart you have when you want to make something happen, is why you are the King you are today. I love that King; even when you feel like you are not where you want to be, you have such authority in your words where you can will it to fruition. Uplift your Queens, speak life into your sons, boost up the egos of your young daughters, and speak respectfully to your mothers.

What are your aspirations as a black man?

As a Black man, I want to be an example to the children coming

up. Expose my children to generational wealth; my children have

me as their model! My son works on cars. After being raised in a

barbershop, my daughter does hair. Instill morals and work ethic

in your children. They look up to you.

~Jeff The Barber~

King,

You have access to words and phrases that have strong ties to the black community, and like everything else we create, they are implemented and twisted by those that don't. Yet, your connection to these words has the power to speak deep down to the King in you, the boy in you left hiding, and the man in you "they" deemed inferior and said you would never amount to. My dear King, when you refuse to speak power over your life and will things into existence, the etymology of the words and the power attached gets lost. Affirm and declare, King, what's yours is already waiting on you, and I can't wait to see it come to life.

SPEAK IT INTO EXISTENCE!

Today's Exercise:

Captivate your words as they will captivate others. Feel the power of the words you speak before they leave your mouth; what you say reflects your thoughts, who you are, and how you see others and yourself. If you speak nasty words to others, it becomes a reflection of you. Speak with caution, love, will, and authority.

SAY THIS OUT LOUD AND BELIEVE IT:

*"MY WORDS ARE COMPELLING,
MY WORDS ARE CAPTIVATING,
MY WORDS ARE INFLUENTIAL."*

DEAR BLACK KING, CHANGE THE NARRATIVE!

My fellow black men, why do we feel if the next man disagrees with you, their opinion is wrong? Why is the disrespect for the black woman at an all-time high? When was the last time you encouraged your fellow black men to do better in life, even if it means passing you up?

~Cory Moore~

Look out for your people. It's easier than you think get out of your egos and

stop competing with one another... don't just live to die."

~Jeff the Barber~

King,

What is essential for you to thrive fully? As a Queen aiming to empower a King, I can attest that it starts here. It begins with releasing the toxicity and anger that eats away at your flesh from the inside out. Self-hate originated from your childhood;

ingrained in you to dislike everything about who you were. To self-hate!!! Whether it was because you looked like your absentee father or reminded someone else of the one, two, or multiple men that have hurt, robbed, killed, or stolen. Regardless of who they are, you break cycles, tear down walls, and transition into a dimension as you advance in life. Even when others can move past, let go and move forward, you have already made the change to stop looking in the rearview and smash the gas!!

King,

I need to see you stand firm. Aside from your mistakes, you show the world how to walk in modesty to right your wrongs. Show them who you are as you walk into purpose and pour into your passion. Show them you are a good father, let them hear the power in your voice and your ability to lead. Put on the many hats you wear and let the sauce drip on the healing you give, your business expertise, artistic expression, and magic you innate. The narrative does not change on its own; you must be the one to…

CHANGE THE NARRATIVE!

Today's Exercise:

Take some time and think about what is holding you back. Is it your thoughts, your environment, or your mentality? How can you be the change you want to see? Make a goal and begin the journey. The change begins with you.

SAY THIS OUT LOUD AND BELIEVE IT:

"I CAN ENCOURAGE,
I CAN MAKE A DIFFERENCE,
I CAN RENOVATE."

DEAR BLACK KING, YOU ARE A BOSS!

"I don't have aspirations to be a boss. As a disclaimer, I have enough knowledge to recognize that being a boss can mean "a position of power in the black community" or associated with "getting money" or employs others, which, in my opinion, are all a bit jaded and skewed. With that, anyone can be a boss, differing on what kind of boss you are seeking to be. Many people have their perception and opinion of what it is to be a "Boss," We as a culture come from and have this deep-rooted mentality where we were conditioned to feel like we don't have authority or power over things we find essential. This is why many people associate money and wealth with being a "boss" instead of being a boss of yourself. Being a boss is not about money or wealth. To me, being a "Boss" means you have power and authority over yourself. You have authority and control over yourself to start making some excellent decisions that can help grow you. If you can create a vision for yourself and a mission that serves others and has growth inside it, that's a F***ing boss!

~Kenneth Ledford~

Dear Black King,

How well, do we know how they pad and label the black man, highlighting your failures and concealing your accomplishments? They put this image in the world that a successful black man is no more than an athlete on a scholarship or a rapper with a record deal. Otherwise, they are drug-dealers and

67

convicts. Black King, you come from the struggle, and you already walked in the trenches; you are all too familiar with pain and suffering, yet you skyrocket past it all. You demand respect and respect others without using derogatory and spiteful words of self-denigration (i.e., my niggah this, my niggah that, or any other nigga/spoken words of self-worth). You come seasoned with power and dignity. A pleasure that is deep-rooted within that reaffirms the majesty of kings from which you came. You are a boss! Not that hood definition of a boss, but you are a boss drawn from "the hood" that transcends through it all because that is what bosses do.

King, be patient and know that sometimes you must go through the worst to get to the best; and you, my love, are the best at whatever it is you do. Stay strong and continue to move forward. You rise in the face of the imbalance, inequality, and persecution. You continue to show up for yourself and those in your circle. You do not aim to get ahead; you are the head. They want you to think that all you will ever do is fade to the bottom of the totem pole, but you are beyond that. You are originators, attorneys, physicians, performers, CEOs of firms, stand up men, fathers, and husbands. You are a real boss, an endowment to humanity, and to those who encounter your unmistakable presence. Black man,

YOU ARE A BOSS!

Today's Exercise:

BOSS UP! NO EXCUSES, NO COMPLAINTS! BELIEVE IN WHO YOU ARE, AND ALL THAT YOU DESIRE IS ALREADY DONE! YOU GOT THIS KING; I BELIEVE IN YOU!

SAY THIS OUT LOUD AND BELIEVE IT:
"I CAME, I SAW, I CONQUERED!"

Dear King,

Give me your hand & trust that I seek the same path you desire—one of purpose & truth.

Give me your friendship, and in me, you will find a true companion—someone who values your mind, body, and spirit without judgment.

Give me your heart & I promise always to be consistent in showing you the real meaning of unconditional love: the freedom to be, the space to manifest, and the peace to coexist.

Shelter me, and I promise to make any place you rest your head a home. Sharing with you the warmth of my presence, the light of my words and the abundance that our connection vs attachment brings.

Give me your seeds & we will both bear the fruits of our labor. Teaching our children the importance of self-awareness, accountability, and independence shows them how to lead healthy, fulfilling lifestyles and become the best version of themselves.

King, you are my leader, my Sensai, and my protector as I am yours. We are one. Nothing in this realm is greater and more vibrational than my love for you. I hold this space for you in both light & dark and dare anything to stand in my way of that. Namaste

~Shaquita Monique~ ∞

Made in the USA
Columbia, SC
05 August 2024

40046265R00045